Teaching Investigative Skills

Book 3
Ages 9–10

Chris Tooley

The author, Chris Tooley, is an Advanced Skills Teacher (AST) working in Cambridgeshire. He has practical experience of working with teachers across a wide range of schools.

Acknowledgements

I would like to offer my thanks to my wife, Joanna, who has been a significant influence in shaping the materials and unstinting in support and encouragement. Also to Shân Oswald, Senior Science Advisor for Cambridgeshire, and all the primary colleagues who played an important part.

© 2003 Folens Limited, on behalf of the author.

United Kingdom: Folens Publishers, Apex Business Centre, Boscombe Road, Dunstable, LU5 4RL.
Email: folens@folens.com

Ireland: Folens Publishers, Greenhills Road, Tallaght, Dublin 24.
Email: info@folens.ie

Poland: JUKA, ul. Renesansowa 38, Warsaw 01-905.

Folens allows photocopying of pages marked 'copiable page' for educational use, providing that this use is within the confines of the purchasing institution. Copiable pages should not be declared in any return in respect of any photocopying licence.

Folens publications are protected by international copyright laws. All rights are reserved. The copyright of all materials in this publication, except where otherwise stated, remains the property of the publisher and authors. No part of this publication may be reproduced, stored in a retrieval system, or transmitted, in any form or by any means, for whatever purpose, without the written permission of Folens Limited.

Chris Tooley hereby asserts his moral right to be identified as the author of this work in accordance with the Copyright, Designs and Patents Act 1988.

Editor: Rebecca Harman
Layout artist: Lee Williams
Cover design: Duncan McTeer
Cover image: Digital Vision
Illustrations: Jean de Loren

First published 2003 by Folens Limited.
Reprinted 2003.

Every effort has been made to contact copyright holders of material used in this publication. If any copyright holder has been overlooked, we should be pleased to make any necessary arrangements.

British Library Cataloguing in Publication Data. A catalogue record for this publication is available from the British Library.

ISBN 1 84303 016-0

Contents

Introduction iv
Background vi

Skill session: Forming Questions 1

Forming Questions OHT 1–OHT 5

Forming Questions Pupil Sheet 8

Practical session:

What affects how quickly washing dries? 12
An application of Forming Questions

Skill session: Predictions 14

Predictions OHT 1–OHT 11

Predictions Pupil Sheet 1 27
Predictions Pupil Sheet 2 28
Predictions Pupil Sheet 3 29
Predictions Pupil Sheet 4 30

Practical session:

What affect does excercise have on your pulse rate? 31
An application of Predictions

Skill session: Planning 33

Planning OHT 1–OHT 4

Practical session:

What material is best at muffling a ticking clock? 39
An application of Planning

Resources:

Planning Card 41

Planning Sheet 43

Pupil Investigation Booklet after 44

Introduction

The materials in this book form the third part of the foundation skills for scientific enquiry at Key Stage 2 and develop the skills learned in Years 3 and 4.

Skills sessions

Lesson plans, OHTs and Pupil Sheets for the following topics:
- Forming Questions
- Predictions
- Planning.

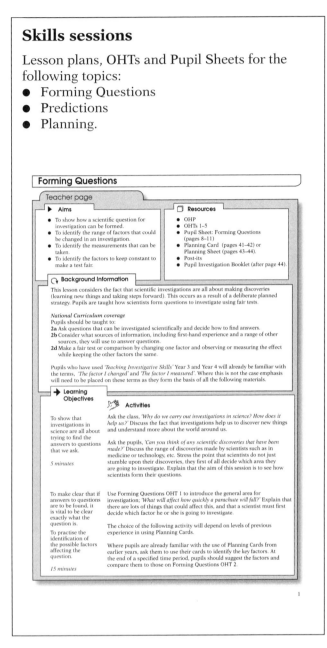

Pupil Sheets

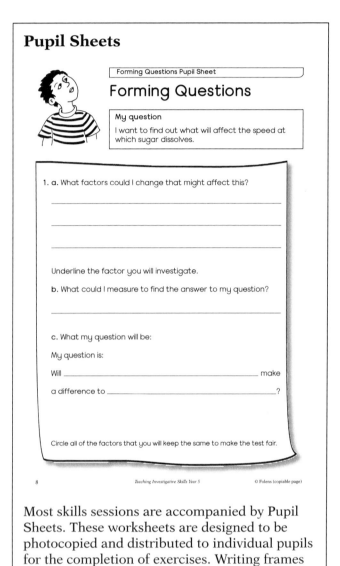

Most skills sessions are accompanied by Pupil Sheets. These worksheets are designed to be photocopied and distributed to individual pupils for the completion of exercises. Writing frames have been used throughout these worksheets to ensure that pupils are able to concentrate on gaining new investigative skills whilst minimising literacy demands.

Practical application sessions

Each skills session is followed by lesson plans, linked to QCA units, detailing the reinforcement of the skills in an overtly scientific and practical context.

At the end of each lesson plan there is a list of other investigative activities that can be used to further embed the skills. These examples have been drawn from the Year 5 QCA units.

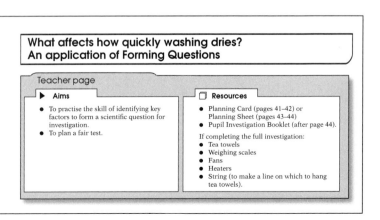

iv

Planning Cards and Planning Sheets

Two discrete resources have been provided to aid the all-important planning process of investigations. Either is suitable for use in the teaching of this skill and all subsequent investigative lessons. However, individual teachers may prefer one or the other format.

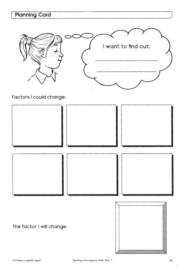

The Planning Card, which can be found on pages 41–42, can be used in conjunction with Post-its to provide pupils with a 'hands on' planning framework for the identification of factors to be investigated. This is best accomplished by photocopying the two pages back to back and then laminating the sheet. This ensures that the cards can be used time after time for any planning activities.

The Planning Sheet, which can be found on pages 43–44, provides a writing frame that pupils can use in two ways. The Planning Sheet can be photocopied and laminated to provide a quick, reusable reference for pupils when writing up an investigation, or the sheet can be photocopied and given to pupils to use as a writing frame, which can be fixed into their science books.

Pupil Investigation Booklet

The Pupil Investigation Booklet for Year 5 can be found after page 44. To construct the booklet, simply photocopy the four individual sheets back to back and then fold and staple the resulting two sheets.

The booklets can be used in two ways:
- In conjunction with the skills sessions to provide immediate reference to the key learning points and writing frames introduced in the session.
- When carrying out any subsequent practical investigations. The booklets provide a single location where pupils can gain help and reminders when encountering any of the taught skills. Pupils should be encouraged to use this resource rather than immediately asking the teacher as, in this way, pupils can be encouraged to develop a personal working understanding of skills, so becoming increasingly independent in their work.

A copy of the booklet can be given to each pupil so that annotations can be added, or class sets can be made and re-used from year to year.

Background

Origins and development

The materials in this book were developed in response to numerous requests from primary colleagues and advisory teachers for a coherent scheme to teach the skills of scientific enquiry (Sc1).

The following skills are focused on:

- Forming questions
- Predictions
- Planning fair tests
- Tables
- Graphs
- Conclusions
- Evaluations.

These specific skills were chosen for a number of reasons:

- To lay a sound foundation of skills for primary pupils to interact with the scientific knowledge and understanding required at Key Stage 2.
- To reflect the emphasis on Sc1 in the end of Key Stage National Curriculum assessments.
- To enable pupils to approach investigative work with confidence at Key Stage 2 and beyond.

The initial materials, aimed at Year 6 classes, were trialled in a group of over 35 schools. Responses from teachers were positive and further modifications were made to include Year 5. This scheme was then adopted by Cambridgeshire LEA and recommended to all primary schools.

The success of this scheme led to calls for the development of complementary materials for Years 3 and 4. These were duly completed and tested in classroom trials. The whole programme was then revised to form a complete Key Stage 2 scheme.

Classroom trials of the complete Key Stage 2 schemes led to further positive feedback including an OFSTED report that noted, 'this systematic programme is proving an effective foundation for teaching good lessons very sharply focused on scientific skills.'

The nature of the materials

Early discussions with primary school teachers, backed up by a review of published materials, suggested that normal practice for pupils to learn the skills of scientific enquiry was by the following:

- Meeting the skills for the first time within the context of a practical investigation.
- Being asked to deal with several new skills at the same time.

It was found that a more profitable way to introduce these key skills was for pupils to be taught the skills individually and in a context free from the competing 'noise' of practical work. In this way, the skills themselves would take centre stage as the sole learning objective.

Accordingly, each new skill is introduced in a theoretical session, and outlined in a detailed lesson plan using overhead transparencies to communicate new ideas to pupils. Although non-practical, the design of the session and accompanying worksheets has focused upon ensuring that all pupils are actively involved in the learning process.

The application of the skills in practical contexts is vital if pupils are to gain a full understanding of the scientific process. To this end, follow up activities have been developed (referenced to QCA units) to accompany each skills session.

The final components of the materials are the Pupil Investigation Booklets that accompany each year at Key Stage 2. These booklets can be photocopied and used as a first resort, encouraging pupils to develop increasing independence in investigative work.

This structure is most simply described using the diagram below:

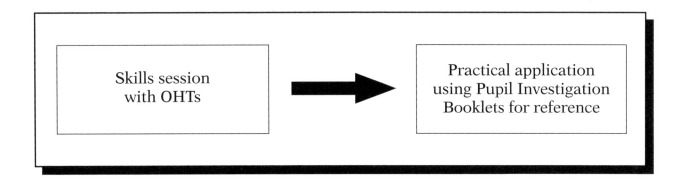

Progression of materials over the key stage

The skills taught in each successive year reinforce and build upon those developed earlier. Years 3 and 4 concentrate on foundation skills, dealing with discontinuous factors (discrete variables), whereas Years 5 and 6 concentrate on the relationships between continuous factors (continuous variables). The culmination of this work comes in Year 6 when pupils are challenged to complete a number of whole investigations. This development can be most clearly appreciated in the table on page viii.

Skill Area	Year 3	Year 4	Year 5	Year 6
Forming Questions	Identifying key factors and introducing the terms, *'The factor I changed'* and *'The factor I measured'*.	Using factors to suggest what will happen in an investigation.	Forming questions for investigation and making predictions.	Using factors to plan fair tests and describing patterns in results.
Predictions	Suggesting the outcomes of a range of circumstances involving discrete factors (variables). Explaining ideas, often using everyday knowledge and understanding.	Making predictions with increasing use of simple scientific facts to explain ideas.	Suggesting the outcomes of a range of circumstances involving continuous factors (variables). Explaining ideas, often using scientific facts.	Making predictions over a range of contexts using scientific facts to justify ideas.
Planning Fair Tests	Identifying the factors to be controlled to make simple, fair tests involving a small number of factors.	With help, planning fair procedures and considering whether tests are fair or not.	Developing clear, step-by-step instructions to fairly investigate questions set by the teacher.	Planning and carrying out fair investigations with increasing independence.
Tables	With help, producing simple tables, mostly involving one series of data.	Increasingly producing simple tables independently (using Pupil Investigation Booklets).	With help, producing tables involving more than one series of data.	Independently producing tables involving more than one series of data (using Pupil Investigation Booklets).
Graphs	With help, producing simple bar graphs.	Producing simple bar graphs with increasing independence (using Pupil Investigation Booklets).	Independently producing simple bar graphs or, with help, line graphs.	With help, producing line graphs.
Conclusions	Saying what was found out in an investigation.	Saying what was found out in an investigation and, increasingly, using simple scientific facts to explain the findings.	Saying what was found out in an investigation and using simple scientific facts to explain the findings.	Identifying and describing patterns found between continuous factors (variables) and using scientific facts to explain these findings.
Evaluations		Looking back at investigative work and suggesting one point that could be improved.	Looking back at investigative work and suggesting two or more points that could be improved.	Considering a whole investigation and suggesting two or more points that could be improved and how it would be done.

Forming Questions

Teacher page

▶ Aims

- To show how a scientific question for investigation can be formed.
- To identify the range of factors that could be changed in an investigation.
- To identify the measurements that can be taken.
- To identify the factors to keep constant to make a test fair.

Resources

- OHP
- OHTs 1–5
- Pupil Sheet: Forming Questions (pages 8–11)
- Planning Card (pages 41–42) or Planning Sheet (pages 43–44).
- Post-its
- Pupil Investigation Booklet (after page 44).

Background Information

This lesson considers the fact that scientific investigations are all about making discoveries (learning new things and taking steps forward). This occurs as a result of a deliberate planned strategy. Pupils are taught how scientists form questions to investigate using fair tests.

National Curriculum coverage
Pupils should be taught to:
2a Ask questions that can be investigated scientifically and decide how to find answers.
2b Consider what sources of information, including first-hand experience and a range of other sources, they will use to answer questions.
2d Make a fair test or comparison by changing one factor and observing or measuring the effect while keeping the other factors the same.

Pupils who have used *'Teaching Investigative Skills'* Year 3 and Year 4 will already be familiar with the terms, *'The factor I changed'* and *'The factor I measured'*. Where this is not the case emphasis will need to be placed on these terms as they form the basis of all the following materials.

➔ Learning Objectives

To show that investigations in science are all about trying to find the answers to questions that we ask.

5 minutes

To make clear that if answers to questions are to be found, it is vital to be clear exactly what the question is.

To practise the identification of the possible factors affecting the question.

15 minutes

Activities

Ask the class, *'Why do we carry out investigations in science? How does it help us?'* Discuss the fact that investigations help us to discover new things and understand more about the world around us.

Ask the pupils, *'Can you think of any scientific discoveries that have been made?'* Discuss the range of discoveries made by scientists such as in medicine or technology, etc. Stress the point that scientists do not just stumble upon their discoveries, they first of all decide which area they are going to investigate. Explain that the aim of this session is to see how scientists form their questions.

Use Forming Questions OHT 1 to introduce the general area for investigation; *'What will affect how quickly a parachute will fall?'* Explain that there are lots of things that could affect this, and that a scientist must first decide which factor he or she is going to investigate.

The choice of the following activity will depend on levels of previous experience in using Planning Cards.

Where pupils are already familiar with the use of Planning Cards from earlier years, ask them to use their cards to identify the key factors. At the end of a specified time period, pupils should suggest the factors and compare them to those on Forming Questions OHT 2.

Forming Questions

Teacher page

→ Learning Objectives

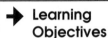 **Activities**

Where pupils are new to this resource, first discuss the pupils' ideas, then use Forming Questions OHT 2 to guide the pupils through the use of the Planning Cards. This is more effective if Post-its are placed over the boxes and revealed as ideas emerge. Introduce the term 'factor'.

To decide on an appropriate factor to change in the investigation.

5 minutes

Using Forming Questions OHT 2, ask the pupils, *'If you were the scientist, which of these factors would you choose to investigate?'*

In making this choice, ask the pupils to consider how practical their suggestions would be to investigate in the classroom. Some factors might be limited by equipment availability. Explain that, wherever possible, pupils should try to investigate factors that can be increased numerically, e.g. the mass on the parachute, rather than the material the canopy is made of. This is because it will allow them to draw a line graph of the results.

Select the amount of mass hung on the parachute as the factor to be investigated.

To identify the factor that could be measured.

5 minutes

Use Forming Questions OHT 3 to consider the factor that will be measured in this investigation. Ask the pupils to think of all the different things they would have to measure in this experiment.

Possible answers include the following:
- The mass of the parachute.
- The height the parachute is dropped from.
- The width of the parachute.
- The time taken for the parachute to fall.

Use Forming Questions OHT 4 to discuss the pupils' answers. Demonstrate that they are trying to identify the specific factor that will answer the question, not the range of factors that they could measure.

To form a question for investigation.

To identify the factors to be controlled to make the test fair.

5 minutes

Use Forming Questions OHT 5 to show pupils how to form a simple question using the writing frame. Refer back to Forming Questions OHT 2 to show that the factors not selected for investigation need to be controlled to make the test fair.

To practise the technique of forming questions.

To appreciate the link between the factors that could be changed and those that will need to be controlled in a fair test.

25 minutes

Ask the pupils to practise these techniques using Pupil Sheet: Forming Questions (pages 8–11) and their Planning Cards (pages 41–42).

Give the pupils 5 minutes to attempt the first example only. Discuss the answers, showing that the factors to be controlled (to make the test fair) are those factors that were identified but were not selected for investigation.

Give the pupils 15 minutes to complete the rest of the Pupil Sheet. Discuss the answers with the class.

Factors I could change:

| The amount of mass hung on the parachute | How big the parachute is | The height the parachute is dropped from |

| The material the parachute is made from | The shape of the parachute | |

The factor I will change:

> The amount of mass hung on the parachute

Forming Questions OHT 2

Investigation question

How does the ………………………………………….of the parachute affect the speed at which it falls?

Our prediction

I predict the parachute which is the……………………………………… will fall more slowly

than………………………………………………………………………………………….I think this because

the………

What we will change

What we will measure

Measurements

Description of parachute	Time taken to fall

There are lots of things that you have to measure in an investigation. You may have thought of some of these:

The mass hung on the parachute

The height the parachute is dropped from

The time taken for the parachute to fall

However, only one of these can tell you the answer to your original question; 'What will affect how quickly a parachute falls?'

Which do you think it is?

The answer is:

The time taken for the parachute to fall

What I am going to change	What I am going to measure
The amount of mass hung on the parachute	The time taken for the parachute to fall

My question is will...

> the amount of mass hung on the parachute

make a difference to...

> the time taken for the parachute to fall?

Forming Questions Pupil Sheet

Forming Questions

My question

I want to find out what will affect the speed at which sugar dissolves.

1. a. What factors could I change that might affect this?

   _____
   _____
   _____

   Underline the factor you will investigate.

   b. What could I measure to find the answer to my question?

   _____

   c. What my question will be:

   My question is:

   Will _____ make

   a difference to _____ ?

   Circle all of the factors that you will keep the same to make the test fair.

Forming Questions Pupil Sheet

My question
I want to find out what will affect the speed at which a towel dries.

2. **a.** What factors could I change that might affect this?

_____

_____

_____

Underline the factor you will investigate.

b. What could I measure to find the answer to my question?

_____

c. What my question will be:

My question is:

Will _____ make

a difference to _____ ?

Circle all of the factors that you will keep the same to make the test fair.

© Folens (copiable page) *Teaching Investigative Skills Year 5*

Forming Questions Pupil Sheet

My question

I want to find out what will affect the number of cress seeds germinating.

3. a. What factors could I change that might affect this?

_____

_____

_____

Underline the factor you will investigate.

b. What could I measure to find the answer to my question?

_____

c. What my question will be:

My question is:

Will _____ make

a difference to _____ ?

Circle all of the factors that you will keep the same to make the test fair.

10   *Teaching Investigative Skills Year 5*   © Folens (copiable page)

Forming Questions Pupil Sheet

My question

I want to find out how high a ball will bounce.

4. a. What factors could I change that might affect this?

_____

_____

_____

Underline the factor you will investigate.

b. What could I measure to find the answer to my question?

_____

c. What my question will be:

My question is:

Will _____ make

a difference to _____ ?

Circle all of the factors that you will keep the same to make the test fair.

© Folens (copiable page)   *Teaching Investigative Skills Year 5*

What affects how quickly washing dries?
An application of Forming Questions

Teacher page

▶ Aims

- To practise the skill of identifying key factors to form a scientific question for investigation.
- To plan a fair test.

Resources

- Planning Card (pages 41–42) or Planning Sheet (pages 43–44)
- Pupil Investigation Booklet (after page 44).

If completing the full investigation:
- Tea towels
- Weighing scales
- Fans
- Heaters
- String (to make a line on which to hang tea towels).

Background Information

This is a part investigation that examines the factors affecting the rate of evaporation; **QCA Unit 5d:** Changing State. The factors affecting the rate of evaporation include the following:
Surface area: the larger the surface area, the faster the drying due to there being a greater surface over which the water can evaporate.
Temperature: the higher the temperature, the faster the drying as there is more energy to evaporate water molecules to become gas.
Amount of wind: the windier it is, the faster the drying as molecules of water vapour are removed from the vicinity of the cloth as soon as they evaporate, effectively leaving space for more molecules to evaporate.

This lesson plan outlines the formation of the scientific question and the development of a fair test. The option to carry out and complete the investigation in full is available.

Where QCA units have been followed pupils will have covered the meaning of the term *evaporation* in a variety of contexts.

➔ Learning Objectives

To identify the factors affecting the drying of damp cloths.

To form a scientific question for investigation.

20 minutes

Activities

Introduce the pupils to the context for the lesson: the school caterers have asked you to investigate how their tea towels can be dried quickest after drying up all of the school dinner crockery.

Ask the pupils to use a Planning Card (pages 41–42) or Planning Sheet (pages 43–44) to identify the factors that might affect the drying of the cloths.

Possible answers include the following:
- The temperature of the room.
- How wet the cloths were to start with.
- The material the cloths are made from.
- Whether the cloths are folded or spread out.
- Whether the cloths are left in windy or still conditions.

Discuss the factors identified. Decide as a class which factor to investigate. If your intention is to carry out the full investigation (as suggested in the QCA unit) take care to choose an appropriate factor.

Ask the pupils to identify the factor they could measure to decide which cloth dried the fastest. Ask them to form a question using the Planning Card or Planning Sheet and the Pupil Investigation Booklet (after page 44) as reference.

What affects how quickly washing dries?
An application of Forming Questions

Teacher page

 Learning Objectives

 Activities

To identify the factors that need to be controlled to make the test fair. *10 minutes*	Give the pupils 5 minutes to make a list of all the factors that would need to be controlled to make the test fair. Make a list of the pupils' suggestions on the board, reinforcing the fact that the factors to be controlled are the same factors that were identified in the first part of the lesson but were not selected for investigation.
To plan a fair test. *15 minutes*	Ask the pupils to work in groups to plan a set of instructions to undertake a fair test. Challenge the pupils to produce a clear enough set of instructions so that a new pupil arriving at the school next lesson could easily carry out the test.
To critically consider investigative plans. *15 minutes*	Ask one group to read out their plan. Note the plan down on the board. Ask the class to comment on whether any important details have been missed out; is it clear how the test is to be made fair? Add details in another colour to the board. Ask all groups to reconsider their plans and to add in any details that have been missed out.

Further investigations where this skill could be reinforced

QCA Unit 5a: *Keeping Healthy*
What factors might affect the pulse rate?

QCA Unit 5b: *Life Cycles*
What factors might affect the germination of seeds?

QCA Unit 5c: *Gases Around Us*
What factors might affect the amount of air trapped in different soils?

QCA Unit 5e: *Earth, Sun and Moon*
What factors might affect the length of a shadow?

QCA Unit 5f: *Changing Sounds*
What factors might affect the note produced by a plucked string?

Predictions

Teacher page

▶ Aims
- To devise predictions in the form of relationships.
- To base predictions on some pre-existing knowledge.

🗁 Resources
- OHP
- OHTs 1–11
- Pupil Sheets 1 and 2: Predictions (pages 27–28)
- Pupil Sheets 3 and 4: Prediction Practice (pages 29–30)
- Pupil Investigation Booklet (after page 44).

↻ Background Information

This lesson teaches the skill of making justified predictions with continuous variables.

National Curriculum coverage
Pupils should be taught to:
2c Think about what might happen ... when deciding what to do.

The content of this session develops the skills taught as part of the Year 3 book where pupils were taught to say what they thought would happen in an investigation and to provide an explanation. The key to this skill is the understanding of the terms *'The factor I changed'* and *'The factor I measured'* as covered in the Forming Questions session.

→ Learning Objectives

 Activities

To show how a prediction can be constructed using a simple pattern of words.

10 minutes

Remind pupils of the meaning of the term *prediction*. Ask them to predict the answers to some simple questions, such as, *'What time do you think it will get dark tonight? How old do you think this school is? How fast could you run to the playground and back?'*

Use Predictions OHTs 1 and 2 to give a scientific context for introducing a pattern of words for constructing a prediction.

Ask the pupils to identify the factor being changed (the number of batteries) and the factor being measured (the brightness of the bulb). Ask them to try to use the pattern of words provided to come up with a prediction. Discuss the pupils' ideas before using Predictions OHT 3 as an example.

To practise the formation of predictions using a simple pattern of words.

15 minutes

Revise the process of forming a prediction:

1. Identify the factors being changed and those being measured.
2. Put these terms into the pattern of words given.

Ask the pupils to complete the two examples on Predictions OHT 4 using Pupil Sheet 1: Predictions (page 27). Discuss the answers with the class. Ask the pupils to complete the examples on Predictions OHT 5 using Pupil Sheet 2: Predictions (page 28).

Predictions

Teacher page

 Learning Objectives

 Activities

To show that good predictions are based on something that the person knows.

10 minutes

Use Predictions OHTs 6, 7 and 8 to consider the differences between a prediction that is substantiated and one that is not.

Using Predictions OHT 6, ask the pupils to identify the factor being changed (number of bags) and the factor being measured (time taken to walk home). Explain that the answer on OHT 7 is good but lacking in any substantiation (proof). However, the answer gives a reason for the prediction on OHT 8. It is based on something already known.

Ask the pupils to attempt to work out the example given on Predictions OHT 9. Ask them to identify the factor being changed (time spent chatting) and the factor being measured (amount of lunchtime given) before using the pattern of words (provided in the Pupil Investigation Booklet) to make a prediction and to give some explanation of the outcome.

To practise the formation of predictions using the pattern of words taught.

15 minutes

Ask the pupils to make predictions for the examples on Predictions OHT 10 using Pupil Sheet 3: Prediction Practice (page 29). If time allows, ask the pupils to make predictions for the examples on OHT 11 using Pupil Sheet 4: Prediction Practice (page 30). Challenge more able pupils to make their predictions using scientific knowledge rather than everyday knowledge.

To discuss the predictions made by pupils.

10 minutes

Discuss each of the exercises requesting alternative explanations.

I think that when the

is increased/decreased

the

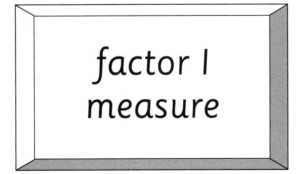

will increase/decrease.

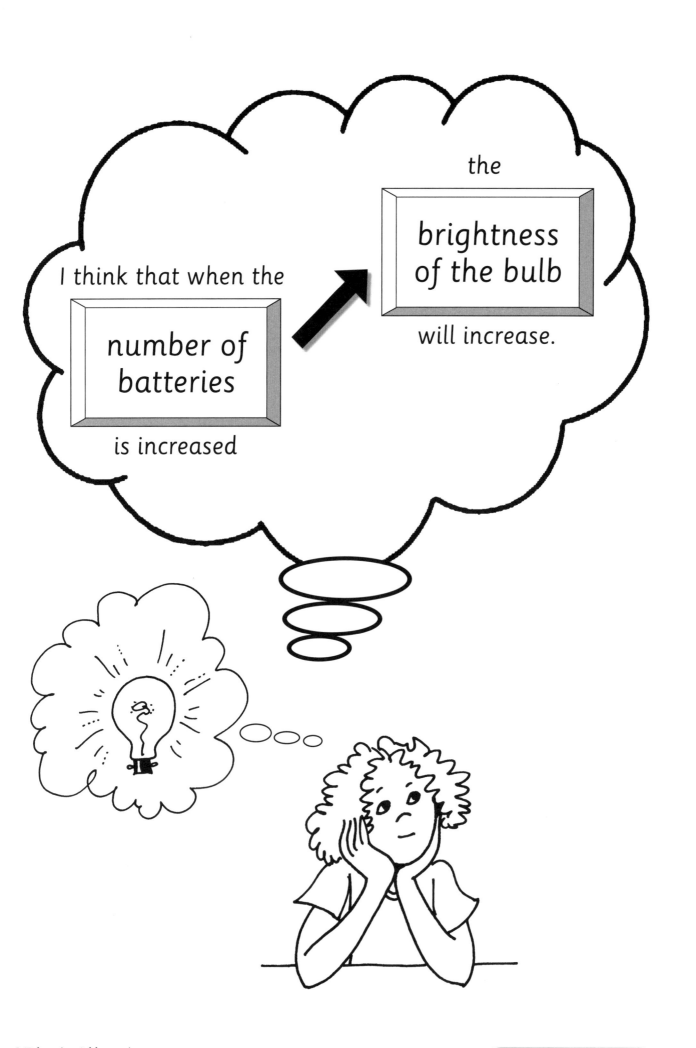

Prediction practice

Try to make some predictions:

1 How will the hardness with which a drum is hit affect the loudness of the bang?

2 How will the mass of a tennis ball affect the height it bounces?

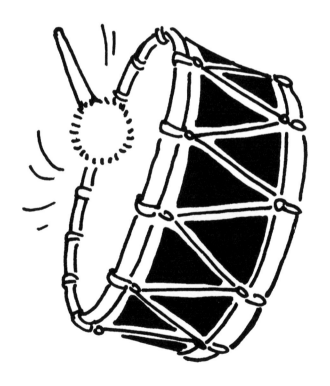

Prediction practice

1 How will the number of spoonfuls of coffee powder affect the strength of a cup a coffee?

2 How will the size of your shoes affect how far you could kick a football?

3 How will the size of a squirrel's mouth affect the number of nuts it could fit into its mouth at once?

How is the time it takes us to walk home from the shops affected by the number of bags we are carrying?

I think that when the number of bags increases, the time taken to walk home will also increase.

What affect will the time you spend chatting in class have on the amount of lunchtime the teacher gives us?

Prediction practice

Write predictions for each of the following questions by:

- Deciding which factor is being changed and which factor is being measured.

- Making a prediction where you say 'what' you think will happen and then 'why' you think it will happen.

1. How will the number of clouds in the sky affect the amount of sunlight that could be absorbed by a plant?

2. How will the amount of air being blown into a balloon affect its size?

Prediction practice

Write predictions for each of the following questions by:

- Deciding which factor is being changed and which factor is being measured.

- Making a prediction where you say 'what' you think will happen and then 'why' you think it will happen.

1 How will the speed at which you complete your class work affect the amount you have to do for homework?

2 Predict how the number of weeds in your garden will affect the time you take to clear it.

3 How will the size of a jam jar placed over a candle affect the time taken for the candle to go out?

4 How will the length a spring stretches be affected by the mass of an object hung from it?

Predictions Pupil Sheet 1

Predictions

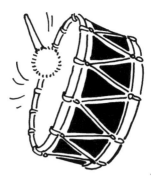

1. The factor being changed is the **hardness with which the drum is hit**.

   The factor being measured is the **loudness of the bang**.

   I think that when the **hardness with which the drum is hit** is **increased** the **loudness of the bang** will

   _____ .

2. The factor being changed is the **mass of a tennis ball**.

   The factor being measured is the **height it bounces**.

   I think that when the **mass of the tennis ball increases** the **height it bounces** will

   _____ .

© Folens (copiable page)   *Teaching Investigative Skills Year 5*   27

Predictions Pupil Sheet 2

1. The factor being changed is the _____.

   The factor being measured is the _____.

   I think that when the _____ is _____ the _____ will _____.

2. The factor being changed is the _____.

   The factor being measured is the _____.

   I think that when the _____ is _____ the _____ will _____.

3. The factor being changed is the _____.

   The factor being measured is the _____.

   I think that when the _____ is _____ the _____ will _____.

Prediction Practice Pupil Sheet 3

Prediction Practice

1. I think that when the _____ is _____ the _____ will _____ .

I think this will happen because I know that _____
_____ .

2. I think that when the _____ is _____ the _____ will _____ .

I think this will happen because I know that _____
_____ .

Prediction Practice Pupil Sheet 4

Prediction Practice

1. I think that when the _____ is

   _____ the _____

   will _____ .

   I think this will happen because I know that _____

   _____ .

2. I think that when the _____ is

   _____ the _____

   will _____ .

   I think this will happen because I know that _____

   _____ .

3. I think that when the _____ is

   _____ the _____

   will _____ .

   I think this will happen because I know that _____

   _____ .

What affect does exercise have on your pulse rate?
An application of Predictions

Teacher page

▶ Aims

- To practise the skill of producing a prediction involving continuous variables.
- To justify a prediction using scientific knowledge.

🗋 Resources

- Stopwatches
- Planning Card (pages 41–42) or Planning Sheet (pages 43–44)
- Pupil Investigation Booklet (after page 44).

↻ Background Information

Pulse rate is a direct measure of how fast the heart is beating. Normal resting heart rate for an adult is 72 beats per minute, in a child it is usually slightly higher. The speed of the heart rate depends on the level of demand for oxygen needed by the body. As exercise occurs, muscles contract to an increasing degree dependent on the level of exercise being undertaken. As demand increases, the heart beats faster to deliver oxygen at the required rate. When exercise ceases the heart rate gradually decreases until it returns to resting rate; **QCA Unit 5a:** Keeping Healthy.

Where QCA units have been followed pupils will have considered the role of the heart in pumping blood around the body and the relationship between heart rate and pulse.

➔ Learning Objectives

Activities

To identify the factors that could affect pulse rate and to form a question for investigation.

10 minutes

Ask the pupils to use a Planning Card (pages 41–42) or Planning Sheet (pages 43–44) to identify a range of factors that might affect their pulse rate.

Possible answers include the following:
- Amount of exercise.
- Amount of food eaten.
- How fit a person is.
- How calm someone is feeling.
- Whether they have just had a shock.
- Whether they have used any medication.

Discuss the answers with the class. Select the amount of exercise as the factor to investigate. Write the fully formed question on the board indicating the factor to be changed and the factor to be measured.

To form a justified prediction.

20 minutes

Devise a plan to investigate how the amount of exercise affects the pulse rate, for example:
1. Measure pulse rate at rest for 1 minute.
2. Carry out gentle exercise for 1 minute.
3. Measure pulse rate again.
4. Carry out vigorous exercise for 1 minute.
5. Measure pulse rate again.

It is important that the type of exercise to be carried out is explicitly described and that account is taken of any medical conditions of pupils.

Ask the pupils to write a prediction of the effect that exercise will have on their pulse rate and to explain their reasoning. Direct pupils to use their Pupil Investigation Booklets (after page 44) for reference if needed.

Discuss the pupils' predictions giving no indication of whether they are right or wrong at this stage.

What affect does exercise have on your pulse rate?
An application of Predictions

Teacher page

 Learning Objectives

 Activities

To carry out the practical investigation and produce a table of results.

10 minutes

Ask the pupils to use their Pupil Investigation Booklets to help them construct a suitable table for the results of this investigation before carrying it out.

To consider the meanings of the results gained.

20 minutes

Ask the pupils to consider whether their predictions were correct or not. Discuss the pupils' results and explain that exercising muscles need an increased supply of blood. You may wish to make the link that blood is carrying oxygen to the muscles, but this is not a requirement of the Key Stage 2 Programme of Study.

Discuss what happens to the pulse rate after exercise has stopped. Ask the pupils to use their new knowledge to justify their ideas. Ask them to write their own explanation of why increased exercise caused the pulse rate to increase.

Further investigations where this skill could be reinforced

QCA Unit 5b: *Life Cycles*
Predict how the brightness of a flower's petals will affect the number of insects attracted to it.

QCA Unit 5c: *Gases Around Us*
Predict which soil will contain most air.

QCA Unit 5d: *Changing States*
Predict how the temperature of a room will affect the speed at which wet cloths dry.

QCA Unit 5e: *Earth, Sun and Moon*
Predict how the time of day affects the length of a shadow.

QCA Unit 5f : *Changing Sounds*
Predict how the pitch of a sound produced by blowing over the top of a bottle can be altered.

Planning

Teacher page

▶ Aim

- To teach pupils that instructions for a practical experiment must be clear and precise.

🗋 Resources

- OHP
- OHTs 1–4
- A pullover
- Pupil Investigation Booklet (after page 44).

↻ Background Information

This lesson teaches pupils the importance of producing clear sets of instructions when planning an investigation. The context used provides a memorable image that can successfully be referred to in later investigations.

National Curriculum coverage
Pupils should be taught to:
2a Ask questions that can be investigated scientifically and decide how to find answers.

➔ Learning Objectives

✋ Activities

To introduce the idea that instructions must be clear if an investigation is to be correctly carried out.

20 minutes

Ask whether anyone in the class has ever helped their mum or dad to bake a cake or bread. Ask one pupil, *'How do you know what to do? How much flour to use? How long to leave in the oven?'* Develop the idea that a recipe is needed to tell you exactly what you need to do in a way that everyone can understand.

Use Planning OHTs 1 and 2 to introduce the pupils to Robbie the Robot. Robbie is quite a clever robot; he understands most of the simple words of the English language, however, he hasn't learnt any skills. Ask the pupils to spend 5 minutes trying to write a list of instructions to teach Robbie how to dress them with a pullover.

When the time is up, ask one pupil to read out their set of instructions. Act out the instructions yourself, dressing a volunteer pupil. Deliberately interpret the instructions literally, for example, if you are told to pick the pullover up, do so with one hand instead of two.

Make the point that pupils need to think very carefully about the instructions before writing them down.

To practise producing a list of clear instructions to describe a series of actions.

20 minutes

Ask the pupils to write instructions for the tasks outlined on Planning OHT 3. Once complete, ask the pupils to work in pairs, reading their instructions aloud to their partner who tries to act out exactly what has been said. Warn pupils that Robbie cannot speak (and so cannot ask or answer any questions).

Planning

Teacher page

Learning Objectives

 Activities

To recap on the ideas introduced and consider why planning has to be completed so carefully.

5 minutes

Ask the pupils why scientists have to make sure that their plans are very clear.

Possible reasons for this include the following:
- If they didn't the results might be wrong.
- Any new scientific discovery is always checked by other scientists who must be able to follow the same instructions.
- Safety hazards might result if, for example, quantities of chemicals were measured out incorrectly.

Ask the pupils to suggest the sorts of things that scientists must include in any investigative plan.

Possible suggestions include the following:
- What the experiment is trying to show or find out.
- What you have to do.
- The equipment you will use.
- What measurements you will take.
- How many times you will repeat the experiment.

To apply the ideas of good planning by critiquing a piece of work.

15 minutes

Use Planning OHT 4 to present pupils with an example of a scientific plan. Ask them to identify any things that are unclear and might lead to problems.

Possible answers include the following:
- No statement of how much Plasticine should be used or where it will be attached to the parachute.
- No statement of the height the parachute must be dropped from or how it will be dropped.
- No indication of the number of times the experiment should be repeated.
- Unclear that a stopwatch will be needed rather than just a watch.

Ask the pupils to check through some of the plans written in each other's science books. Ask them to 'play at being teacher' and write a comment after the piece of work.

- Meet 'Robbie the robot', your new domestic helper.

- Your problem is that Robbie doesn't know how to do even the simplest task. You are going to have to teach him!

- Write a list of instructions to teach Robbie how to put your pullover on you.

- Make sure they are really clear so that Robbie won't get in a muddle!

Now try to write a plan to teach Robbie how to do the following things:

- Draw a straight line that is 10cm long.
- Write the letter E.
- Find the word 'Robot' in a dictionary.
- Sharpen a pencil.

Now try your plans out on your friends!

Here is a plan for an investigation on how the mass carried by a parachute affects the time taken for it to fall.

It was written by a young boy called Chris, aged 9.

Look carefully at his plan and decide what is wrong with it.

1 Take the parachute and put some Plasticine on it to act as a mass.

2 Drop the parachute.

3 See how long the parachute takes to drop using a watch.

4 Write down the time.

5 Add some more Plasticine to the parachute and try it again.

6 Add some more Plasticine again, then pack your things away.

What material is best at muffling a ticking clock?
An application of Planning

Teacher page

▶ Aim
- To plan a clear set of instructions for an investigation.

Resources
- Pupil Investigation Booklet (after page 44)
- Ticking timers
- A variety of materials to test, e.g. bubble wrap, foam sheeting, artificial fur, blanket material
- Metre rules.

Background Information

Sound vibrations can travel through a wide range of materials. However, the ease with which they pass through varies with the particular material. Sound travels faster through solids than liquids, and faster through liquids than gases; **QCA Unit 5f:** Changing Sounds.

Where QCA units have been followed pupils will have met the idea that sounds are caused by vibrations that travel through a wide range of media. They will also have met the idea that some materials are used to deliberately stop sounds, e.g. earmuffs.

➡ Learning Objectives

Activities

Learning Objectives	Activities
To introduce the context for the investigation. *5 minutes*	Explain to the class that the head teacher of your school is planning to have some music practice rooms built. These rooms have to be well sound-proofed so that pupils are able to practice without being disturbed. You have been asked to investigate which material should form the filling for the walls between the rooms. Show the pupils the variety of materials to test.
To devise a fair comparison of the materials. *15 minutes*	Show the pupils a ticking clock as a source of sound with which to test the sound-proofing materials. Ask the pupils to work in groups to devise a fair way to test the materials' sound reducing qualities. Possible plans might include the following: • Putting a single thickness of material around the clock and measuring the distance away from the clock that the ticking can no longer be heard. • Sitting a set distance away from the clock and adding more and more layers of a certain material until the sound can no longer be heard. Discuss the pupils' plans and decide whether they would be a fair test or not. Agree on the range of strategies that could be used.
To write a clear plan for the investigation. *15 minutes*	Ask the pupils to write out their plans as a series of clear and precise instructions. Give them a time limit for completion.

What material is best at muffling a ticking clock?
An application of Planning

Teacher page

 Learning Objectives

 Activities

To check the accuracy of the plans. *5 minutes*	Ask the pupils to swap lists of instructions and to check whether the instructions are clear enough to be easily carried out.
To carry out a fair test. *5 minutes*	Ask a pupil to read out their plan with other pupils carrying out the instructions. Record the results on a results table on the board.
To discuss the conclusions that can be drawn from the results. *5 minutes*	Ask the pupils to look at the results and to make their recommendation of the best material to use for sound-proofing the new music practice rooms.

Further investigations where this skill could be reinforced

QCA Unit 5a: *Keeping Healthy*
Plan an investigation on which pupil in the class has the strongest finger muscles.

QCA Unit 5b: *Life Cycles*
Plan an investigation on the factors needed by seeds to germinate.

QCA Unit 5c: *Gases Around Us*
Plan an investigation on which type of gas moves through the air quickest.

QCA Unit 5d: *Changing States*
Plan an investigation on the effect of wind on the drying of a wet cloth.

QCA Unit 5e: *Earth, Sun and Moon*
Plan an investigation on how the direction of a shadow changes during the course of a day.

Planning Card

I want to find out:
_____
_____

Factors I could change:

The factor I will change:

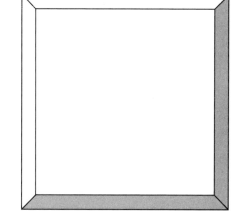

© Folens (copiable page)   *Teaching Investigative Skills Year 5*   41

Planning Card

What I am going to change

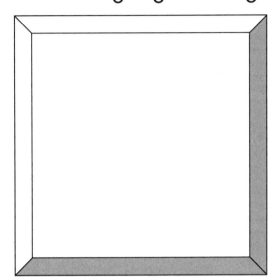

What I am going to measure

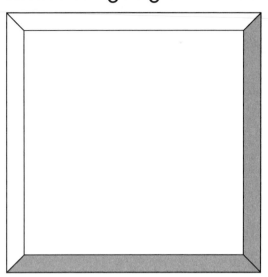

My question is will...

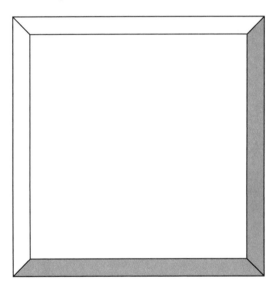

make a difference to...

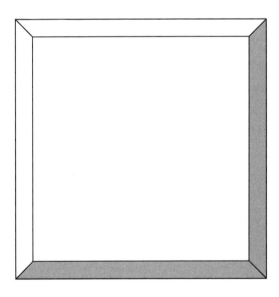

Planning Sheet

1. a. What I want to find out:

   _____

   _____

   b. What factors **could I change** that might affect my question? Make a list:

   _____

   _____

   _____

   Underline the factor you will investigate.

   c. What **could I measure** to find the answer to my question? Make a list:

   _____

   _____

What my question will be:

My question is:

Will _____ make a

difference to _____ ?

Circle all of the factors in **b.** above that you will keep the same to make the test fair.

HOW TO CREATE ...
Your Guide to Science Investigations Booklet

STEP 1
Photocopy the title page.

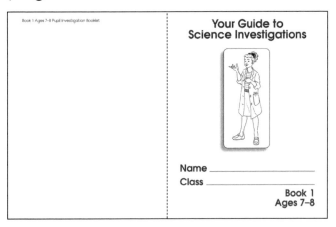

STEP 2
On the back of the title page photocopy pages 2 and 7.

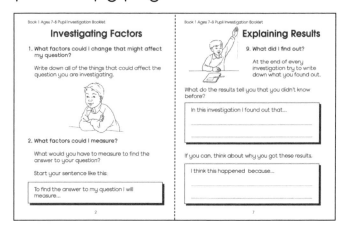

STEP 3
Photocopy pages 6 and 3.

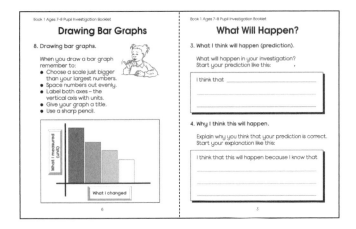

STEP 4
On the back of pages 6 and 3 photocopy pages 4 and 5.

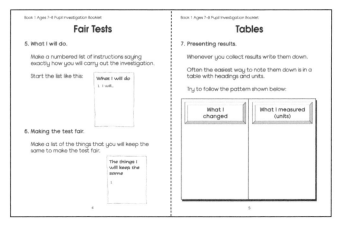

STEP 5
Put the copied sheets together to make the booklet.

Staple if necessary.

Your Guide to Science Investigations

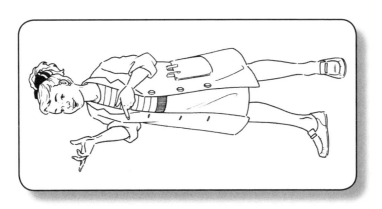

Name _____

Class _____

Book 3
Ages 9–10

Book 3 Ages 9-10 Pupil Investigation Booklet

Forming Questions

1. What factors could I change that might affect my question?

   Write down all of the things that could affect the question you are investigating.

2. What factors could I measure?

   What would you have to measure to find the answer to your question?

   Start your sentence like this:

   To find the answer to my question I will measure...

3. What will my question be?

   My question is will the [factor I change] make a difference to the [factor I measure?]

   2

Book 3 Ages 9-10 Pupil Investigation Booklet

Evaluations

11. How good was my investigation?

    a. Was the question being investigated clear?
    b. Was the test fair?
    c. Were the results noted down clearly?
    d. Is there anything wrong with the conclusion?
    e. Is there anything else that is missing in this report?
    f. What would you change to make the test better?

    7

Book 3 Ages 9–10 Pupil Investigation Booklet

Predictions

4. What I think will happen.

What will happen to what you are measuring when you change the factor (thing) you are investigating?

Use the example below to help you:
I think that when the **factor I change** is (increased, decreased) the **factor I measure** will (increase, decrease).

5. Why I think this will happen.

Explain why you think that your prediction is correct. Start your explanation like this:

I think that this will happen because I know that _____

3

Book 3 Ages 9–10 Pupil Investigation Booklet

Explaining Results

10. What did I find out?

At the end of every investigation try to write down what you found out.

What do the results tell you that you didn't know before?

In this investigation I found out that... _____

If you can, think about why you got these results.

I think that this happened because... _____

6

Planning

6. **What I will do.**

   Make a numbered list of instructions saying exactly how you will carry out the investigation.

7. **Making the test fair.**

   Make a list of the things that you will keep the same to make the test fair.

8. **Presenting results.**

   Whenever you collect results write them down. Often the easiest way to note them down is in a table with headings and units.

   Try to follow the pattern shown below:

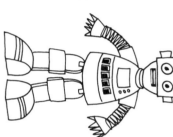

What I changed	What I measured (units)

Drawing Bar Graphs

9. **Drawing bar graphs.**

   When you draw a bar graph remember to:

   - Choose a scale just bigger than your largest numbers.
   - Space numbers out.
   - Label both axes with units.
   - Give your graph a title.
   - Use a sharp pencil!

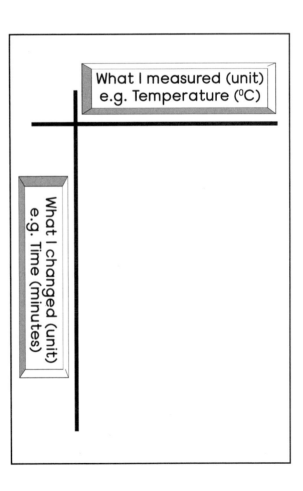